Christmas Together in
Switzerland

Christmas Together in
Switzerland

Christmas Around the World
From World Book

World Book, Inc.

Chicago

Staff

Executive Committee
President
　Jim O'Rourke
Vice President and Editor in Chief
　Paul A. Kobasa
Vice President, Finance
　Donald D. Keller
Vice President, Marketing
　Jean Lin
Vice President, International Sales
　Maksim Rutenberg
Director, Human Resources
　Bev Ecker

Editorial
Director, Digital and Print Content
　Development
　Emily Kline
Editor, Digital and Print Content
　Development
　Kendra Muntz
Senior Researchers
　Lynn Durbin
　Karen McCormack
Administrative Assistant, Digital and
　Print Content Development
　Ethel Matthews
Manager, Contracts & Compliance
　(Rights & Permissions)
　Loranne K. Shields

Editorial Administration
Senior Manager, Publishing
　Operations
　Timothy Falk

Graphics and Design
Senior Art Director
　Tom Evans
Senior Visual Communications
　Designer
　Melanie Bender
Coordinator, Design Development
　and Production
　Brenda Tropinski
Senior Cartographer
　John M. Rejba
Media Editor
　Rosalia Bledsoe

Manufacturing/Production
Production/Technology Manager
　Anne Fritzinger
Senior Production Manager
　Jan Rossing
Proofreader
　Nathalie Strassheim

Marketing
Director, Direct Marketing
　Mark R. Willy
Marketing Analyst
　Zofia Kulik
Marketing Specialist
　Anisha Eckert

World Book, Inc.
180 North LaSalle Street
Suite 900
Chicago, Illinois 60601 USA

Christmas Together in Switzerland
ISBN: 978-0-7166-0833-2

World Book wishes to thank the following individuals for their contributions to this book: Sascha Brawer, Sarah Figlio, Dianne Kiefer-Dicks, Sara Schödler, Katie Sharp, and Brigitte Shidrawi. A previous version of this book was published with the title *Christmas in Switzerland*.

For information on other World Book publications, call **1-800-WORLDBK (967-5325)**, or visit our website at **www.worldbook.com.** For information on sales to schools and libraries, call **1-800-975-3250 (United States),** or **1-800-837-5365 (Canada).**

Printed in China by Shenzhen Donnelley Printing Co., Ltd.,
Guangdong Province
1st printing September 2016

*Previous spread:
A view of the Swiss resort town of Zermatt beneath the imposing Matterhorn.*

*Table of contents:
Historic buildings in Bern illuminated on a winter's night.*

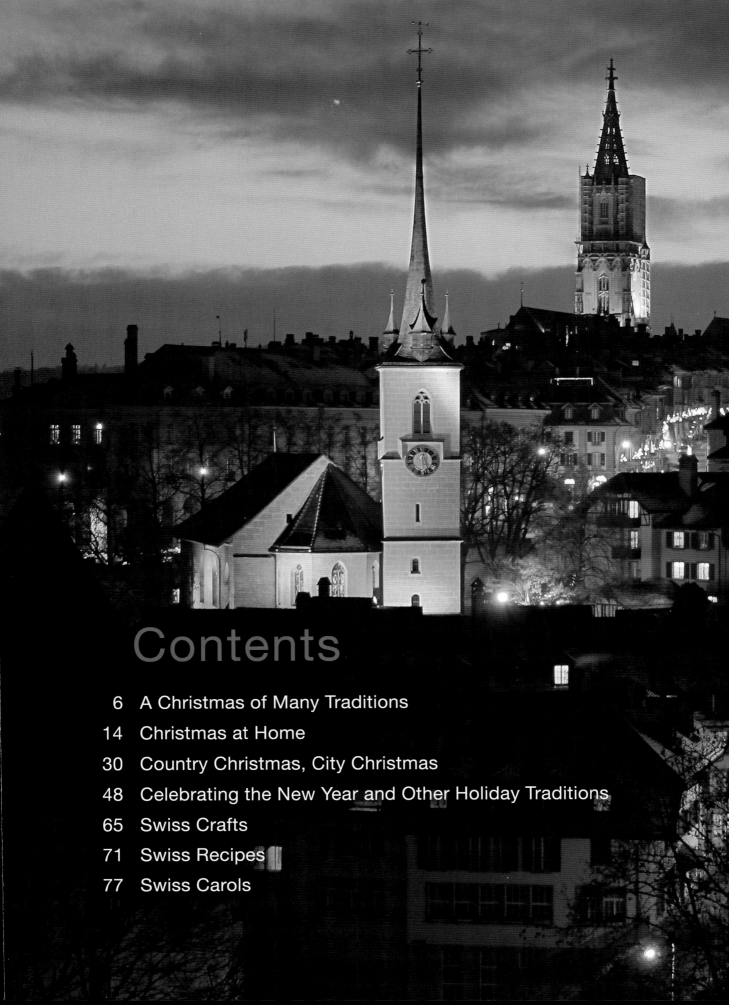

Contents

A Christmas of Many Traditions

Switzerland, a small country tucked in the heart of central Europe, is a place where winter holiday traditions thrive. From boisterous, masked winter processions to quiet Christmas Eve celebrations at home, the holiday season in Switzerland is a charming blend of old and new; Catholic and Protestant; and German, French, and Italian influences. Indeed, the traditions of this holy holiday as it is celebrated in Switzerland demonstrate the true diversity of the people who call this remarkable country home.

While Switzerland is a land of diverse people, there's one thing on which they all can agree: There's no place like their homeland to enjoy the festivities of winter, whether it's sharing a sleigh ride, celebrating Christmas, or welcoming the New Year.

Die Schweiz. Suisse. Svizzera. This trio of official names for Switzerland reflects not only the country's three official languages—German, French, and Italian—but also its multilingual and multicultural identity. Along with these languages, a small percentage of Swiss people speak yet another—Romansh, which has been designated a national language. But the Swiss are diverse not only in language; their religious beliefs differ, as well. About 40 percent are Roman Catholic and 35 percent are Protestant. About 5 percent of the Swiss people are Muslim.

Despite their cultural differences, the people of the 26 cantons (political divisions) and half-cantons that comprise the nation of Switzerland take pride in their country. Today, Switzerland is notable chiefly for its long tradition of neutrality, as well as its almost legendary cleanliness and order and, of course, its high standard of living.

Shared traditions

While Christmas in Switzerland is rich in tradition, it is safe to say that no single "typically Swiss" Christmas tradition exists. The people of each region celebrate the season in their own way. In the past, the country's mountainous landscape discouraged people's awareness of customs in other regions. Today, more borrowing is taking place. A closer look at the Swiss holiday customs and traditions also reveals that many of them have been influenced over the years by neighboring countries.

By far the majority of the Swiss—about 70 percent—speak a form of German called *Schwyzerdütsch* (Swiss-German). Swiss-German-speaking citizens live in the country's northern, eastern, and central cantons. In the west, French is the dominant language, spoken by about 20 percent of the Swiss. Southern Switzerland is home to the 4 percent of the population whose first language is Italian. Romansh-speakers, who make up less than 1 percent of the Swiss population, live in the mountain valleys of the canton of Graubünden in Switzerland's southeast. Romansh is a Romance language that is a mixture of Latin, Italian, and German.

Although certain traditions, such as the Advent wreath, the Christmas tree, and St. Nicholas, are observed by most of the Swiss, each region tends to vary its emphasis. For example, some regions, especially the north and central Swiss-German-speaking Catholic ones, celebrate the beginning of the Christmas season with a visit from St. Nicholas, or *Samichlaus*, as he is called in the Swiss-German dialect, on December 5 and 6. Dressed in a long red robe, carrying a crosier, or shepherd's crook—symbol of a bishop's care for his people—and accompanied by his frightening sidekick, Schmutzli, St. Nicholas brings sweets, nuts, tangerines, and other small treats to the children who have been good. Naughty children must beware, however. The mean-spirited Schmutzli totes a large sack in which to haul them

Christmas trees and snowmen are beloved symbols of the season throughout Switzerland. Here, a man returns from choosing his family's Christmas tree in the Bernese Alps, assisted by his alert dog. A suitably costumed snowman indicates his breathtaking surroundings.

Unity in Diversity

Switzerland is a country of many different people and cultures. Brought together more than 700 years ago in a pact to defend one another, the Swiss relish their diversity and take pride in their unity. The citizens who comprise the different regions of Switzerland have adopted and nurtured their ways of life from their German, French, and Italian ancestors. And they defend these ways of life in the same spirit of independence that has made Switzerland famous.

The country of Switzerland lies just east of France and is less than 1 percent as large as the contiguous states of the United States. Today about 8,300,000 people call this country home, although most family trees branch out to other countries. In fact, Switzerland has a higher percentage of foreign-born residents than any other European country. Most of the Swiss live on a plateau that extends across the middle of the country between the Swiss Alps and the Jura Mountains. Switzerland's richest farmland is in this region, as are most of the large cities and manufacturing indus-

National languages of Switzerland

German | Italian
French | Romansh

tries. The Swiss Alps cover about 60 percent of Switzerland, but less than a fifth of the people live there. The most populated cities of Switzerland include Zurich, Geneva, Basel, Lausanne, and the country's capital, Bern.

The Swiss have a long history of defending their freedom. During the 1200's, the Habsburg family controlled much of Switzerland. Fearing the family's growing power, the free men of what are today the cantons (states) of Schwyz, Uri, and Unterwalden joined forces. In 1291 the three regions declared their freedom and vowed to help defend each other against foreign rulers. Their pledge was the beginning of the Swiss Confederation. The confederation came to be known as Switzerland, taking its name from the canton of Schwyz.

By the 1400's Switzerland became a strong military power and fought several wars in an effort to gain land. In 1515, however, the Swiss suffered a crushing defeat at the hands of the French. Switzerland soon adopted a policy of neutrality, which was eventually guaranteed by the Congress of Vienna (1814-1815).

In 1848, Switzerland adopted the Swiss Constitution, which was revised in 1874. The Constitution established a federal republic in which political powers are divided between the central government and the governments of the 23 cantons—3 of which are divided into half-cantons. The cantons' and half-cantons' independence is ensured by the Constitution. They are real states, each with its own constitution, legislatures, executives, and judiciaries. Legislative power rests with the Swiss people or with a parliament elected by them. So even the cantons, as with almost all aspects of Swiss culture, are united in diversity.

An Advent wreath is a focal point in Swiss churches during the season before Christmas.

off. In other parts of the country, though, especially Protestant ones, St. Nicholas makes fewer appearances.

Even from family to family, holiday traditions vary. Protestant households tend to celebrate Christmas with less fuss and ceremony than do Catholic households. Moreover, in many families the parents come from different language regions, so the traditions have become even more blended. Add to this pattern the texture of the numerous ancient folk customs kept alive throughout the country—Switzerland perhaps leads all other modern Western nations in the number of folk traditions it has preserved—and a marvelous tapestry of holiday celebration emerges. It is this very variety that can be said to be typically Swiss.

But for all the differences in language and custom, a number of Christmas traditions are quite similar throughout Switzerland. Some of these are the Advent wreath, the Christmas tree, Christmas carols, gift giving, a mouth-watering meal either on Christmas Eve or Christmas Day, and sacred church services.

Throughout Switzerland, children count the days until Christmas on Advent calendars. The most common kind of Advent calendar is a small poster with 24 "windows," one to open on each day from December 1 until Christmas Eve. Hidden inside each window is a special Christmas picture, or perhaps a piece of chocolate. Some Swiss buildings have been decorated as giant Advent calendars, with the different scenes created in their real windows. The people in some towns and neighborhoods even turn their homes into a giant Advent calendar. Different families decorate one window in their house with an Advent calendar scene, keeping it hidden from the outside world until their assigned day in December.

Christianity arrives in Switzerland

The celebration of the birth of Christ on December 25 probably began in the Roman Empire around A.D. 326. One of Switzerland's most beloved patron saints, St. Gall, was responsible for bringing

Christianity and the celebration of Christmas to Switzerland in the early A.D. 600's. And although the worship of Christ eventually replaced veneration of the old gods and goddesses, Switzerland is no different from the rest of northern Europe, in that many of its Christmas traditions are adaptations of pre-Christian customs. The ancient custom of decorating the home with greenery to symbolize fertility in the dead of winter, for example, survives in the form of the Christmas tree and the hanging of branches of holly and mistletoe. Singing and gift giving were also part of these pre-Christian celebrations. Even a number of characteristics of St. Nicholas can be recognized in stories of the Norse God Odin or Wotan. According to myth, Odin, who wore a long, white beard, lived for most of the year in his distant dwelling place called Asgard. Every December 21, accompanied by the spirits of the Viking heroes, Odin would sweep back to Earth on his white horse and spirit away misbehaving children. The youngsters, perhaps in hopes of getting on his good side, would leave offerings of food for Odin's horse and his ghostly companions.

Christmas and the Protestant Reformation

The changes in religious doctrine brought about by the Protestant Reformation of the 1500's are among the important reasons why there is such variety in the Christmas celebrations of Switzerland. While the Roman Catholic Church was content to adapt pre-Christian rites and ceremonies for Christian purposes, the reformers, including Ulrich Zwingli in Zurich and, later, John Calvin in Geneva, would have none of that. Among their objections to the Catholic expression of religion in general was its reliance on icons and symbols, which the reformers considered at best superstitious, and at worst, downright sinful. As Protestantism spread through many parts of Swiss-German and French-speaking Switzerland, various aspects of the Christmas celebration were downplayed by the new church. Even today, Christmas celebrations in regions of Switzerland that are chiefly Protestant tend to be quiet family affairs, while St. Nicholas celebrations and the more exuberant masking tend to occur chiefly in Catholic regions.

Christmas at Home

Knowing that someone is Swiss does not necessarily reveal a lot about how he or she spends this winter holiday. Does the family celebration center around the nativity scene, or is the Christmas tree more important? Who brings the gifts—Father Christmas, Samichlaus, the *Christkindli, Père Noël,* the *Gesú Bambino*—and when does the gift-bearer arrive? In some ways the children of Switzerland are the luckiest in the world, because so many kind-hearted spirits stand ready to shower them with treats and presents during the holiday season.

A cottage home in the canton of Graubünden glows with the spirit of Christmas.

As in much of the Christian West, Christmas is an important festival in Switzerland, accounting for seemingly endless hustle and bustle and preparation. The high point of the celebration takes place on Christmas Eve, when children may be spirited out of the house or banished to a side room while their parents adorn the Christmas tree in secret.

The Swiss Christmas tree, unlike the American version, is often illuminated with real candles rather than strings of electric light bulbs. Gold and silver garlands twinkle on the branches, and multihued ornaments add color. Cookies, nuts, fruit, foil-wrapped chocolates, and small presents also hang from the boughs. A star representing the Star of Bethlehem often tops the tree, though some families prefer to reserve that spot for an angel, representing the

Colorful glass ornaments depicting the symbols of the season hang from the boughs of the Christmas trees in many Swiss homes.

Christkindli, a guardian angel thought to protect the household and the nativity scene. In fact, in some parts of Switzerland, it is the Christkindli who delivers the Christmas Eve presents.

Lots of eating, merrymaking, and visiting are also characteristic of Christmastime throughout Switzerland. The Swiss do not have a typical Christmas dinner that is enjoyed by most people, like turkey and dressing in the United States or roast goose in the United Kingdom. Instead, a number of dishes top the list of Swiss favorites. A longtime favorite is fondue, a mixture of any number of cheeses, most often Emmentaler (the "holey" cheese Americans know as Swiss cheese) and Gruyère; a splash of schnapps (kirsch); and white wine. Into this cheese sauce diners dip cubes of bread speared on long-handled forks. Increasing in popularity are two variations on fondue: *fondue chinoises* and *fondue bourguignon,* in which pieces of beef are cooked in hot broth and hot oil, respectively. Rösti, a potato dish similar to hash browns, is served throughout Swiss-German-speaking Switzerland.

Many families eat a light meal on Christmas Eve, often consisting of sliced cold meats, vegetable salads, patés, and tarts. They then indulge in a fancy dinner at midday on December 25. Although Christmas Eve is usually a family affair, friends and relatives may gather on Christmas Day for a meal and hours of visiting and merrymaking.

Protestant and Catholic churches alike celebrate Christmas Eve midnight services, which are always well attended.

St. Nicholas makes his rounds

In the Catholic areas of Switzerland, children mark the beginning of the Christmas season on December 6—St. Nicholas Day. Known as Samichlaus in the Swiss-German-speaking regions, San Nicola or Babbo Natale among Italian-speakers, and Père Noël by those who speak French, St. Nicholas dons a few different guises. Sometimes he

Wearing an outfit much like that donned by the North American Santa Claus, St. Nicholas of Switzerland surprises children at a holiday market.

St. Nicholas and his frightful companion, Schmutzli (right), who awaits his chance to bundle up a naughty child, plan their visit to a village beyond this snowy forest. The generous visitor delivers all kinds of Christmas goodies, including a variety of cookies, fruits, and nuts.

is dressed in a red coat and sports a long white beard similar to the American Santa Claus. And sometimes he is dressed in his bishop's garb with a miter, a tall pointed hat, atop his head and a shepherd's crook held firmly in his grip. His mode of transportation also varies. He may arrive either on foot or riding on a donkey. In Lugano in the canton of Ticino, St. Nicholas has even been known to arrive in the piazza, or town square, on a motorcycle or in a helicopter!

Some communities arrange for St. Nicholas to appear in such public places as the town square or a department store. Sometimes, he even pays a visit to children's homes. When he arrives, mom or dad will often slip him a note outlining the children's offenses and accomplishments, so that he can scold or praise them appropriately. It is not unknown for his grim companion, Schmutzli, to threaten to bundle up naughty children in his bag or swat at them with a broom; but it is all in fun. Good little children sing a song or recite a poem for St. Nicholas, who rewards them with a bag of goodies. And as an added incentive to good behavior in the coming year, he may leave a bundle of switches tied with twine for mom and dad.

Those children who do not receive personal visits from St. Nicholas still benefit from his generosity. In some areas, youngsters leave their shoes outside and in the morning find them filled to the brim with all kinds of Christmas goodies.

Christmas Swiss-German style

"Schöne Weihnachten" can be heard at Christmastime in the streets and homes of Switzerland's northern and central cantons, where Swiss-German is spoken. Specifically, this region consists of the cantons of Aargau, Bern, Glarus, Lucerne, St. Gallen, Schaffhausen, Schwyz, Solothurn, Thurgau, Uri, Zug, and Zurich; the half-cantons of Nidwalden, Obwalden, Basel-Landschaft, Basel-Stadt, Appenzell Ausserrhoden, and Appenzell Innerrhoden; the eastern parts of the cantons of Fribourg and Valais; and much of the canton of Graubünden. The Swiss-German-speaking region also includes three of Switzerland's five major cities: Basel, Bern, and Zurich. The landscape of this region varies from the Jura Mountains in the northwest, across the rich farmland of the Swiss Plateau, to the mighty Swiss Alps.

In Swiss-German-speaking households, the Christmas season begins with the lighting of the first Advent candle on the fourth Sunday before Christmas. The family places an evergreen wreath decorated with small Christmas ornaments and four candles on the dining room table or a coffee table. The family gathers on each of the four Sundays of Advent to light one of the candles on the Advent wreath and sing Christmas carols. Lucky children may receive a little bag of nuts, tangerines, and other goodies. And parents and children have been known to take this opportunity to get in a few hours of *basteln*, or making handicrafts, such as nativity figures, straw Christmas ornaments, or candles.

Many Swiss children also have Advent calendars, with 24 little win-

Christmas means only one thing to some Swiss: cookies and other confections! And luckily there are always plenty to go around. On the list of favorites are Tirggel, molded honey cookies that truly are edible works of art. Above, a baker's stand in the Montreux Christmas market.

dows—one for every day in December up through Christmas Eve. On each day, they open a new window and are treated to a Christmas picture, or sometimes even a candy treat.

Swiss pastries are justifiably renowned, and *Weihnachtsguetzli*, or Christmas cookies molded into different shapes, are one of the centerpieces of the Swiss Christmas season. The Swiss-German-speaking regions lay claim to the most varied assortment and well-known of the Christmas cookies. Many cooks start baking early, a month or so before Christmas, to concoct the array of wonderful treats that will be enjoyed by the family and shared generously with friends and visitors. Shop windows also begin to fill with *Guetzli*, or cookies, packed in festive tins, boxes, and baskets.

Läbchueche (lasting cakes), *Läckerli* (little licks), and *Biberli* (little beavers) belong to a family of spiced honey-cookies related to the German *Lebkuchen*. Some Läbchueche are topped with little paper pictures called *Läbchuechebilder* with such seasonal images as Sam-

ichlaus, a Christmas tree, or a heart with an evergreen branch. Läckerli are flavored with orange peel, and Biberli are filled with a paste of ground almonds, lemon zest, and sometimes, kirsch.

Änisbrötli, little anise breads, start with anise-flavored dough pressed into molds carved with designs of Alpine flowers, such as edelweiss and gentian, or elaborate landscapes. These are similar to the traditional *Tirggel,* abundant in the Zurich area and said to be a descendant of specially prepared honey cakes offered as a gift to the gods in ancient religious ceremonies. Many people so treasure the designs on Tirggel that instead of eating them, they hang them on their walls or the Christmas tree as decorations.

Some popular Swiss cookies are associated with their place of origin. *Basler Brunsli* (Basel brownies) are spiced chocolate and hazelnut cookies often shaped as hearts. *Mailänderli*—so named because a gift of them was once made centuries ago to the duke of the Italian city of Milan—are golden sugar cookies traditionally cut into rounds and scored with parallel grooves. No spices compete with the rich flavor of butter and egg yolks. Other Guetzli are as noteworthy for their fanciful names as for their deliciousness. *Spitzbuebli,* or naughty boys, are shortbread jam-filled sandwich cookies dusted with powdered sugar. *Schenkeli,* crispy oblong fried cookies, get their name— lady's thighs—from their plump shape, as do *Totebeinli*—dead legs. Totebeinli are small, hard hazelnut bars.

A ribbon-wrapped stack of crispy Basler Läckerli.

Children in Swiss-German-speaking Switzerland begin their preparations for Christmas early, making their gift requests to ensure a satisfying haul on Christmas Eve. Some children slip a note to St. Nicholas during his early December rounds. Others leave their lists on the windowsill for Christkindli to pick up during the night. The angel signals its receipt of the message by leaving a chocolate treat behind. The more practical children prefer to entrust their wish lists to the Swiss postal system. Each year, Swiss Post receives thousands of letters addressed to Samichlaus, Père Noel, or even Gesù Bambino. A special team of employees reads each letter and sends a reply to the child who wrote it, provided the writer includes a return address. The envelope of each reply displays a special Christmas stamp.

All the preparations finally lead to Christmas Eve, generally the climax of the holiday celebration in Swiss-German-speaking Switzerland. On that evening, the Christmas tree in all its illuminated splendor, put up in carefully guarded secret by the parents, is revealed to the children. And at long last the eager youngsters are allowed to open their gifts.

Some families of the region choose to remember their departed loved ones on Christmas Eve by making a visit to the cemetery. There they place on the gravesites pine boughs or special decorations that are sold especially for this occasion.

Joyeux Noël: Christmas the French way

Geneva, Jura, Neuchâtel, and Vaud are the cantons that many French-speaking Swiss call home. The cantons of Fribourg and Valais are bilingual, with about two-thirds of the population in each speaking French and about one-third speaking Swiss-German.

Unlike France itself, French-speaking Switzerland welcomed the church reforms of the 1500's, so this region, except for Fribourg, is overwhelmingly Protestant. Throughout most of the region, December 6 comes and goes without much notice. St. Nicholas's and Schmutzli's roles are played by Père Noël, or Father Christmas, and Père Fouettard, respectively. Père Noël climbs through the window on Christmas Eve to leave presents for good little boys and girls. With his red jacket lined with fur, white beard, and round tummy, Père Noël resembles the North American Santa Claus more than St. Nicholas does.

In some families, the children are treated to a personal visit from Père Noël. Before he hands out the presents, the children must display their talents by singing a song, reciting a poem, or playing a musical instrument. And lest the children forget the importance of

Tasty Treats on the Bough

Through the centuries, chocolate has assumed a special place in Swiss life. This holds true even at Christmastime, when chocolate treats are given as gifts and used to decorate the home. Some merchants even sell colorful foil-wrapped chocolates molded in the shapes characteristic of the season and equipped with a small loop to make it easy to hang them on the Christmas tree.

Fine chocolate is as closely associated with Switzerland as fine watches and fine cheese. Switzerland may have risen to its position as one of the world's premier suppliers of chocolate because of three conditions: the Swiss sweet tooth, its long tradition of dairying, and its high standards of quality for everything it produces.

However, the Swiss did not invent chocolate—they only perfected it. The confection probably arrived in Switzerland in the final years of the 1600's, when Bürgermeister Heinrich Escher of Zurich returned home with the news of a delicious drink (an early version of hot cocoa) he had sampled in Brussels. The first Swiss chocolatier was François-Louis Cailler, who opened a chocolate factory in Vevey on the northeast shore of Lake Geneva in 1819. At that time and in the years to come, chocolate was consumed only as a beverage. That changed in 1847, when a British company discovered how to make solid "eating chocolate."

Sometime during this period, Rodolphe Lindt of Bern improved on the rather gritty, slightly bitter eating chocolate available at the time. He came up with a smooth, creamy chocolate that melted in the mouth. But the real breakthrough in chocolate came in Vevey in 1876 when Henri Nestlé teamed up with Daniel Peter, whose in-laws were the renowned chocolatiers, the Caillers. Peter devised a way to add condensed milk, which Nestlé had invented, to chocolate to make milk chocolate.

Today, the Swiss people are the world's largest consumers of chocolate, with a yearly per person consumption of about 20 pounds (9 kilograms). And while surely some of this munching does go on during the Christmas season, an array of Christmas cookies gives chocolate a run for its money during this festive time of year. At any rate, with the sweet, creamy treats dangling on the Christmas tree, no doubt in danger of melting in the warmth of dozens of candles, the urge to rescue the edible ornaments from a gooey demise must be great indeed!

good behavior throughout the year, Père Noël leaves behind a bundle of twigs bound with twine as a reminder of the consequences of being naughty.

In other households, Père Noël comes and goes secretly. On Christmas Eve, the children are allowed in the living room to admire the tree, beautifully decorated but noticeably bare of presents. Then the children are ushered out again as the parents open the window to ease Père Noël's entrance. A little while later, the children are invited back into the living room, where their presents await them. Although Père Noël is no longer there, having slipped quickly out after doing his cheerful chore, the children may still be required to put on a little performance before the present-opening can begin.

Christmas in Ticino

Cross the Alps through the St. Gotthard Pass or the San Bernardino Pass and there lies the canton of Ticino, where many things are noticeably different. Here and there, palm trees and mimosa—with its tiny blossoms and feathery leaves—replace pines, and German and French give way to Italian. In Christmas customs as well, there is a slight shift in emphasis. Although most families put up a Christmas tree, it is the nativity scene, or *presepio*, that plays the most cherished role in the celebration. The tree and the presepio generally go up at the same time. Out of storage comes the little stable made of twigs or wood, and family members embark on outdoor expeditions for moss to line the manger. When that is done, they place figurines of the Madonna, Giuseppe (Joseph), and the sheep, mules, and other animal guardians. Children sometimes make angel figurines at school during holiday time, and those take their place in the presepio as well. Now all is ready for the arrival of the Gesú Bambino, the baby Jesus, whom the family will lovingly add to the presepio at midnight on Christmas Eve.

The churches of Ticino all display presepios, too. In some parishes, it is traditional for teenagers to collect the moss and other adornments and assemble the presepio. In others, the priests take on this important task.

St. Nicholas is San Nicola or Babbo Natale in Italian-speaking Switzerland, and he makes his usual rounds, handing out small goodies on December 6. But the children of Ticino receive their special presents on Christmas Day, and many believe that it is the Gesú Bambino who leaves them. Some thoughtful children put out a bowl of milk or other refreshment for him before they go to bed on Christmas Eve.

The Ticinese enjoy their main Christmas meal on the afternoon of Christmas Day. Italian specialties such as *polenta*, a corn-meal mush; a braised beef dish called *brasatto*; and *risotto*, a rice dish, in a variety of forms are among the favorites.

Ticino, the southernmost Swiss canton, is the warmest part of the country. But even here, snow occasionally graces the branches of the native palm trees.

*Skaters in Lucerne
test their abilities
surrounded by
holiday lighting.*

Holiday in Graubünden

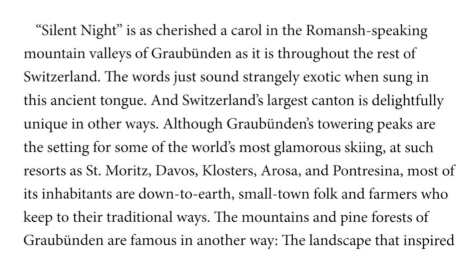

*Quaida not, sencha not
regna pôs dapertuot.
Be a Bethlehem vagliand
staun ils genituors urand
sper luch cher iffaunt.*

"Silent Night" is as cherished a carol in the Romansh-speaking mountain valleys of Graubünden as it is throughout the rest of Switzerland. The words just sound strangely exotic when sung in this ancient tongue. And Switzerland's largest canton is delightfully unique in other ways. Although Graubünden's towering peaks are the setting for some of the world's most glamorous skiing, at such resorts as St. Moritz, Davos, Klosters, Arosa, and Pontresina, most of its inhabitants are down-to-earth, small-town folk and farmers who keep to their traditional ways. The mountains and pine forests of Graubünden are famous in another way: The landscape that inspired the beloved children's tale *Heidi* was the mountainsides above the small town of Maienfeld in the north.

The Engadine Valley in the far eastern part of the canton is the heart of Romansh-speaking Switzerland. At Christmastime, evergreen branches spill from the windowsills of the traditional houses—stout stuccoed homes of several stories with heavy, wooden, arched Etruscan-style doorways—and gold ribbons decorate the wrought-iron door handles. Many of these old houses are covered with designs in an ancient style of etching known as *sgraffito*. Sgraffito designs are made by coating dark gray stucco with a layer of whitewash and then scratching away the whitewash so the dark under layer shows through. Some houses list all their inhabitants—sometimes spanning 300 years. Others are decorated with rosettes, pinwheels, braided

Graubünden, Switzerland's largest canton, is unique in many ways. Majestic snow-capped mountains serve as the backdrop to traditional homes that are often decorated with sgraffito etching.

ropes, and other abstract patterns.

Graubünden is perhaps the single most diverse canton in a country known for its diversity. Romansh, whose several dialects are spoken by about 15 percent of Graubündners, is only one of the canton's native languages. In the north, which borders on Austria and Liechtenstein, the people speak Swiss-German. The region on the south and east, cradled by Italy, is home to Italian speakers.

Graubünden's Christmas traditions reflect this diversity. Some children wake up on Christmas morning to discover their presents from the Christkindli, who visits on Christmas Eve. Others enjoy a visit from St. Nicholas and Schmutzli on December 6, as well. In Catholic towns, St. Nicholas comes dressed as a bishop, while in Protestant towns, he is called *Sontgaclau* and bears the terrifying image associated with Schmutzli elsewhere. Children often receive presents from aunts, uncles, and other relatives on Christmas Day.

For sharing the songs of the season, strolling Swiss carolers may be offered Churer Zimmetstern, star-shaped cinnamon cookies.

As in Ticino, most of the families of Graubünden decorate with both a Christmas tree and a nativity scene, which is known here as a *purseppen*. Each family prepares its own traditional menu for the Christmas meal, often featuring ham or the regional specialty, *Bündnerfleisch*—air-dried beef or game meat pressed into rectangular loaves and served in paper-thin slices. Hospitality reigns supreme at holiday time in Graubünden, as in other regions of Switzerland. In Graubünden homes, guests are always greeted with a bowl of Christmas treats, including *Churer Zimmetstern*, star-shaped cinnamon cookies with a sweet meringue glaze that originated in Graubünden's capital of Chur and hard, white anise-flavored cookies called *Chräbeli*.

One of the best ways to experience Graubünden's stunningly

Red-painted train carriages of the Glacier Express add Christmas color to a scene of blue-white mountain splendor.

beautiful winter scenery is by taking a train ride through its high mountains and deep gorges. Some structures along the route, such as the graceful arches of the 213-foot- (65-meter-) high Landwasser Viaduct, are works of art in themselves. In 2008, the United Nations Educational, Scientific and Cultural Organization (UNESCO) named the Rhaetian Railway in the Abula/Bernina Landscapes to its World Heritage List for amazing architectural and engineering achievements in harmony with the surrounding landscapes. The 42-mile- (61-kilometer-) long Albula railroad line and the 40-mile- (61-kilometer-) Bernina line each have dozens of tunnels, viaducts, and bridges. Both local trains and special scenic trains, such as the Glacier Express and the Bernina Express, use the tracks, which were designed and constructed about 100 years ago.

Country Christmas, City Christmas

Writers often describe Switzerland as a country of small communities. Traditionally, the Swiss have cherished that characterization. In fact, it has been said that the village symbolizes the Swiss identity as a union of independent communities, voluntarily joined together for mutual benefit. Although today the number of families who farm for a living has declined, the Swiss village still thrives. It is these smaller communities that do much to keep traditional Christmas customs a vital part of Swiss culture.

Even Switzerland's major cities are small by modern standards. The largest, Zurich, has a population of only about 373,000. However small, Switzerland is still a modern, cosmopolitan country, and its cities, as others the world over, put on their finest displays during the Christmas season.

The streets of Zurich glimmer like gold during the season of Christmas.

Beloved country customs

Like nearly every other aspect of Swiss identity, there is no "typical" Swiss village. In the Berner Oberland, a highland region in west-central Switzerland, farm families, their hired help, and their cows traditionally lived in large, slope-roofed farmhouses. Ticinese village homes are made of stones of granite, and in the wine-making region around Lake Geneva, the villages are nestled among sweeping vineyards.

Christmas is especially meaningful in Swiss rural areas—especially in the mountain villages—for Christmas church services are often one of the few times during the year that the whole community gathers. The mountain-dwellers descend from the snowy slopes, some on foot, others on skis, still others on sleds drawn by horses jangling with bells. These Christmas gatherings offer an opportunity for extended families to renew connections with the help of the warm spirit of the season.

Perhaps so moved by these church services, a Swiss composer by the name of Paul Burkhard wrote a beautiful play for the church in his home village of Zell, a small community near Zurich. The play, entitled *D'Zäller Wiehnacht (A Christmas in Zell,* also known in English as *A Swiss Nativity),* is performed hundreds of times in several different places each year. The song that is perhaps the best-known Swiss Christmas carol comes from this play. In English, it is called "The Star of Bethlehem Shines Bright."

In the rural communities of Switzerland, people once held to old Christmas superstitions. For example, on Christmas Eve the woman in the family would pick the most perfect onion from the larder. She would cut that onion in half and remove 12 cuplike sections, which she would fill with salt. She would then line them up to represent the 12 months of the year. In the morning, the family could see what the coming year's weather would be: The onion sections containing dry salt foretold dry months, while those with damp salt showed which months would be rainy.

Other folk superstitions concerned farm animals, which were supposed to attain the ability to speak for one hour on Christmas Eve

before the clock struck midnight. People avoided their farm animals during this hour, because disaster or even death was the fate of the human eavesdropper. Clipping the wings of chickens on Christmas Eve, according to those with a superstitious mind, kept them out of harm's way from foxes and other predators all year long. And tying straw around all the fruit trees during Christmas week was said to ensure a plentiful harvest the next year.

Brave souls who wanted to know how many more years they would live could find out on Christmas Eve by opening a Bible at random and pointing to a chapter. The number of verses in the chapter told them the number of years they had left. And young people liked to safeguard their chances for future marital bliss by drinking from nine different fountains in their village as the Christmas Eve church bells rang. When they finished this ritual, they hurried to the church steps, where, it is said, their future spouse would be waiting.

The church is at the heart of Christmas in small Swiss villages, where whole communities gather together.

Celebrating St. Nick

The celebration of St. Nicholas Day takes on a different form in the streets of Switzerland's towns and villages than it does in the homes. In various communities throughout Swiss-German-speaking Switzerland, the holiday brings out the partier in everybody. People don elaborate headdresses and masks and hoist giant bells to pay noisy homage to the beloved saint.

The village of Küssnacht in the canton of Schwyz puts on a well-known celebration called *Klausjagen*, or the pursuit of St. Nicholas, on the evening of December 5. Hundreds of participants dress in white bishop's robes and wear huge bishops' miters (tall, pointed hats), called *Iffele*, constructed of heavy cardboard. Abstract decorative patterns—rosettes, stars, crosses—are cut into the miters, and the holes are covered with colored tissue paper. Lights inside the towering headpieces make a beautiful display of color reminiscent of stained-glass windows. A small group of paraders blows horns while larger groups—sometimes including hundreds of participants—ring huge cowbells, which they swing from thigh to thigh. A crew of *Geisselchlepfer,* or whip-crackers, adds to the noise. These men and boys crack long whips in rhythmic unison. The deafening din is sure to banish any evil spirit lurking in the village streets for the year to come.

The people of Hallwil, in the canton of Aargau, put on a similar show, which they call the *Chlauswettchlöpfe,* a St. Nicholas Day whip-cracking contest. Winners are awarded a pewter pitcher, and six qualified crackers—boys 13 or 14 years old—get to take part in the *Chlausjage* the next day. The six play the part of spirits who visit homes to reward the well-behaved children with gifts and warn the naughty children that they had better shape up.

In the Zurich suburb of Wollishofen, a red-coated St. Nicholas leads a parade of teenagers called *Wollishofer Kläuse* (Nicholases of Wollishofen). Like their kindred spirits in Küssnacht, the Wollishofer Kläuse wear white robes and illuminated headdresses.

Children are responsible for the St. Nicholas procession in the villages of the canton of Glarus. Each village has its own particular style of celebrating the *Klausschellen,* or ringing of cowbells for St. Nicholas. But generally speaking, the custom involves going out sometime during a day or evening around December 6, ringing the ever-popular giant cowbells, and begging for treats door-to-door. This custom is said to have originated in the 1700's, when the first big industries were emerging and children of working-class families were allowed to beg for handouts at Christmastime. Today, it is all in fun, and any child, regardless of the family's economic status, can join the festivities.

The city of Fribourg puts on a special St. Nicholas Day celebration with a slightly more cosmopolitan flair. The event has a special significance because St. Nicholas is the patron saint of the city and canton of Fribourg. Nestled on the bluffs above the Sarine River, Fribourg is an ancient city on the frontier between Swiss-German- and French-speaking Switzerland. It is a truly bilingual city, with street

A Swiss Pilgrimage

Einsiedeln, situated in a valley of the Alps between Lake Zurich and Lake Lucerne, has been a center for pilgrimages for more than a thousand years. What causes people of all ages and from all over the world to journey to this small village in the canton of Schwyz? A carved wooden image of Mary, the mother of Jesus, called the Black Madonna.

The Benedictine monastery of Einsiedeln was founded in the A.D. 800's when Meinrad, a monk, chose this place to live in solitude. The abbess of Zurich gave him a picture of Mary, the Virgin Mother, for which Meinrad built a chapel. The story has it that when Meinrad was murdered in A.D. 861 by thieves, two ravens, who had befriended Meinrad, followed the treasure-seekers to Zurich and shrieked over their heads until they were caught. Soon a monastery was built over Meinrad's grave, and as the ceremony to consecrate the monastery began, a voice was heard. It said three times, "Brother, desist: God himself has consecrated this building."

Over the years the monastery of Einsiedeln was destroyed five times by fire, but the Black Madonna was always rescued unharmed.

The revered Black Madonna of Einsiedeln, here dressed in sumptuous robes, stands above a display of flowers and lighted candles.

When pilgrimages to the wooden image peaked in the 1600's and 1700's, construction of the present-day beautiful baroque church and monastery area began. Today the buildings are considered to be among the finest examples of baroque architecture in Switzerland. The Black Madonna is kept in the Gnadenkapelle (Chapel of Grace), a black marble chapel inside the church.

Even today Einsiedeln remains a focus for religion and culture. While pilgrimages are still popular the year around, many people make their journey in winter to view the Bethlehem Diorama, a representation of the manger in Bethlehem with 500 carved wooden figures, that stands near the square outside the abbey.

signs in both Swiss-German and French and a population generally fluent in both tongues. During the 1500's, Fribourg also remained firmly Catholic, while the rest of the region went the way of Calvin and the other Protestant reformers.

St. Nicholas (or Père Noël in French), astride his donkey and accompanied by his sidekick Schmutzli (or Père Fouettard), leads a procession through the streets of the old city. As he makes his way, he greets the children and hands out nuts, tangerines, and Biscômes, spiced buns in the shape of St. Nicholas. Eventually he arrives at a raised stage erected in front of the Cathédral St. Nicholas. There he addresses the crowd with a humorous summarization, in both French and German, of the local events of the past year.

Holy Night celebrations

St. Nicholas Day is for boys in Hallwil, but on Christmas Eve and Christmas Day, seven 13- to 14-year-old girls play the starring roles. One girl, dressed all in white and her face hidden by a veil,

Visitors to the winter sport centers of Switzerland have been known to take part in the fine art of ice sculpture. The results are as grand as the artisans' imaginations, as evidenced by this tower of barnyard animals.

Men wearing towering hats and large bells on straps around their necks process solemnly in the Nünichlingler. The marchers are lead by a bearded man who waves a pole to bat away malicious spirits.

impersonates the Christmas Child, or *Wienechtchind*. Accompanied by six attendants wearing rose-colored robes, the Wienechtchind visits as many homes in the village as time allows, silently greeting the families inside with a handshake and passing out treats to the children. After the six attendants sing a carol, the group silently departs.

Another somewhat solemn Christmas Eve celebration takes place in Rheinfelden, a town east of Basel on the Rhine. There, 12 members of the Brotherhood of St. Sebastian participate in the *Brunnensingen* (fountain-singing), a procession that has taken place since 1541 in remembrance of the plague of 1348. Dressed in somber funeral attire and wearing tall black hats, the 12 visit seven fountains in turn. At each fountain, they sing a carol, pausing when God or Christ is mentioned in the song to doff their hats in praise. When they have finished their circuit, they attend midnight Mass together.

Another Christmas Eve procession that involves men in hats takes place in Ziefen in the canton of Basel. The *Nünichlingler* is so called because it involves the ringing of bells (*chlingle*) at 9 p.m. (*nüni*). Thirty or more young (and until recently, only unmarried) men dress up in dark coats and wear towering black top hats. Without saying a word, they proceed with dignity through the town, ringing their bells rhythmically. The tallest man in the group wears a white beard and leads the parade, representing a mean-spirited Samichlaus. He carries a long pole from the end of which a sooty rag dangles. Until the

1950's, the man used the rag to frighten and anger people by smearing soot on them and their houses and scaring away winter demons. Today this curious display is a playful and harmless competition among those in attendance.

City celebrations

Swiss cities all have their own special charm. Bern, the capital, has its nearly 600-year-old sandstone arcades that stretch for miles; Zurich, wealthy, sophisticated, and glittering, boasts lovely views of Lake Zurich and the Limmat River; Geneva appears chic yet proper on the shore of Lake Geneva; Basel, historically a center of culture and learning, but also a busy port on the Rhine River, receives thousands of international commuters each day; and Lugano, with its Mediterranean flair, shows off its mountain landscape, palm trees, and blooming gardens.

Many cities throughout the world put on their holiday finest at Christmastime, and Swiss cities are no exception. Towering

Metal trees aglow with Christmas lights branch out over the Limmat River in the city of Zurich.

evergreen trees in city squares shine with colored lights. Zurich's Bahnhofstrasse, considered one of Europe's most fashionable shopping districts, is ablaze with lights hung in long vertical strands that cascade over the streets like drapery, suggesting the glow of the northern lights. One evening each December, hundreds of candles bob gently down the Limmat River during the traditional Lichterschwimmen event in Zurich. The candles float in tiny paper boats made by schoolchildren in the canton, a way for them to wish everyone a Merry Christmas.

A special treat for the children of Zurich is the Märlitram. Samichlaus drives this gaily decorated antique trolley, while the young passengers listen to Christmas stories. Other towns have similar rides, which are often sponsored by local stores.

The streets of Swiss towns are also warmed by the joyful sound of caroling. Swiss-German-speaking Lucerne, Rapperswil, and Wettingen have the best-known gatherings of *Sternsinger,* or star singers, who proceed through the streets during Advent carrying

Zurich's Bahnhofstrasse, considered one of Europe's most fashionable shopping districts, lives up to its reputation, especially at Christmastime. Strands upon strands of tiny lights cascade over the streets, while the hustle and bustle of the season takes place below.

illuminated stars representing the Star of Bethlehem. Accompanying the singers are the Three Wise Men and Mary, Jesus, and Joseph. The canton of Graubünden has a rich tradition of holiday singing. In Romansh-speaking communities such as Celerina and Samedan in the Engadine Valley, adults and children start caroling around five o' clock on Christmas Eve. Later in the evening, teenagers carrying candles lend their voices to the choir.

In mid-December, the people of Geneva pause from their Christmas preparations to honor a special event in the city's history. Escalade (French for *scaling the walls*) celebrates the city's defeat of the French Duke of Savoy in December 1602. The Genevans, inspired by the preaching of reformer John Calvin, had become Protestants during the 1500's. The duke tried to capture the city and return it to Roman Catholicism. As the story goes, a housewife called Mère Royaume leaned out a window and dumped a pot of steaming soup

All aboard! A gaily decorated antique trolley car, known as the Marlitram, rolls around the streets of Zurich during the holiday season. Much to the delight of children, Samichlaus himself sometimes serves as driver. Two angels tell Christmas stories to children during the trip.

Basel's version of the Christmas market—a special seasonal event in many Swiss cities and towns.

on soldiers trying to climb the city walls. Her quick thinking raised the alarm, and the city fought off its attackers.

Highlighting the modern celebration of the Escalade are the three-legged *marmites*, or soup kettles, made of chocolate and filled with marzipan vegetables. Traditionally, families smash the pots and eat the sweets after Saturday night dinner on the weekend of the Escalade.

The public celebrations include races through streets of the Old City on the first Saturday of December. The main events take place on a weekend in the middle of the month. The town becomes a live-action history lesson with reenactments of the scaling of the old city walls, demonstrations of period weapons, and singing by children. A parade of Genevans dressed in period costumes and bearing torches is accompanied by a herald on horseback, who pauses from time to time to proclaim the Genevans' victory over the Savoyards.

Shopping for Christmas

Shopping is just as much a part of Christmas in Switzerland as eating and merrymaking. A Swiss Christmas market is the perfect place to take a stroll, sample yummy Christmas treats, and find the perfect gift. Cities and towns throughout Switzerland organize markets, some for the entire season and others for just a weekend or two. Most markets are outdoors, in city squares or along picturesque cobblestone streets. In the evenings, shoppers can sip hot chocolate beneath twinkling lights and visit the wooden stalls, called *chalets*, of dozens of merchants. Ornaments sparkle. Handcrafts may include fine wood carvings and hand-dipped candles. In the brisk winter air, displays of woolen scarves and sweaters look especially inviting. Food chalets offer gingerbread, chocolates, and pastries, as well as heartier sausages and soups.

Revelers can stock up on Leckerli—a spiced cookie—at Basel's historic Läckerli-Huus (Leckerli House).

Some Christmas markets feature a giant Christmas tree, an ice rink, or other attractions. The town of Montreaux at the eastern end of Lake Geneva has a large Christmas market. In addition, the nearby Châteaux de Chillon hosts a medieval Christmas market on several weekends, complete with costumed musicians, dancers, storytellers, and craftspeople.

There are also indoor markets, such as those set up in Zurich's main train station. In fact, a big city like Zurich often has Christmas markets in a number of locations.

Swiss cities also have plenty of shops in which to find that perfect gift, buy decorations, or simply enjoy the sights and the smells of chocolates, cinnamon, and sweets. In Zurich's old town, Niederdorf, stands Conditorei Péclard im Schober (Péclard Cake Shop at Schober). The building that houses this bakery and cafe was built in 1340 and has housed cafe shops for more than 100 years. While

Escalade

Ask a Genevan how Christmas is celebrated in that city, and the reply may be a dignified, "Christmas here is a quiet, private affair. We don't make a big ruckus. After all, the Reformation put an end to a lot of unnecessary religious fuss." True enough, the Protestant Reformation caught on like a brushfire with Calvin's inspired preaching at Cathèdrale-St-Pierre, and even today, the refined Puritan simplicity of the now-Protestant church is a fitting symbol for the Genevan distaste for anything too rollicking.

Except, of course, for Escalade.

The *Escalade* (French for "scaling the walls" and not to be confused with a Cadillac model of SUV!) comes right in the middle of the holiday season. The celebrations start with races through the streets of the Old City on the first Saturday in December. The main events occur on a weekend in the middle of the month. The town becomes both the site of a live-action history lesson and a big party. Included in the events are reenactments of the scaling of the old city walls, demonstrations of period weapons, and singing by children dressed in costume. The celebration

Escalade Marzipan Vegetables

7 oz. almond paste*
3 tbsp. light corn syrup
1/2 tsp. vanilla extract

1 - 1 3/4 cups sifted confectioners' sugar, separated
food coloring

Place almond paste in a medium mixing bowl. Using a fork, break up almond paste into small pieces. Add corn syrup and vanilla extract; mix thoroughly. Add 3/4 cup of the powdered sugar, 1/4 cup at a time, until mixture forms a smooth, stiff dough. Continue adding powdered sugar a little at a time, kneading dough until it is no longer sticky. Color and shape small balls of marzipan into vegetables or other figures as desired.

* Available in the baking section of most grocery stores

Genevans dressed in period costume take to the streets in mid-December to celebrate Escalade, which recognizes the defeat in 1602 of the French Duke of Savoy. The festivities culminate at St. Pierre, where participants gather in the glow of a bonfire and rejoice in song.

culminates with Genevans pouring noisily into the streets to celebrate the defeat in 1602 of the French Duke of Savoy, whose lineage had ruled Geneva for many generations and who was trying to recapture the city and turn it back to Catholicism. Dressed in period costumes and bearing torches, paraders proceed through the city streets accompanied by a herald on horseback, who pauses from time to time to proclaim the Genevans' victory over the Savoyards. The celebration ends at St. Pierre, where the happy Genevans sing patriotic songs and bask in the glow of a large bonfire.

Although the realistic battle reenactments are true crowd-pleasers, one of the highlights of the occasion, especially for the children, is the three-legged marmites, or soup kettles, made of chocolate and filled with marzipan vegetables. No good Genevan home is without one at this time of year. The marmite plays a major part in the Escalade celebration because, as the story goes, when

the Savoyard soldiers were making their assault on the city walls, a housewife called Mère Royaume leaned out the window and dumped a pot of steaming soup on the attackers. She then heaved the pot onto the head of one, killing him. Her quick thinking raised the alarm that the city was under attack. And while each family celebrates in its own way, traditionally after the Saturday-night family dinner during Escalade, the youngest person present smashes the chocolate marmite, declaring *"Ainsi périrent les ennemis de la République!"* ("Thus perish the enemies of the Republic!").

always a pleasant place to shop and enjoy a steaming cup of hot chocolate and a pastry, at Christmastime the cafe's gift boutique is the place to find holiday nostalgia and the perfect gift for someone with a sweet tooth.

Basel, located in the far northwest corner of Switzerland on the borders of France and Germany and divided by the Rhine River, is home to a couple of well-known shops that are open the year around, but whose wares are most appropriate at Christmastime.

The first is the Johann Wanner Christmas House, which is perhaps best known for its impressive assortment of glass Christmas ornaments. Located in Basel's medieval old town, the store is jammed with Christmas trinkets and supplies of all kinds, including cards, lights, tinsel, strings of beads, chocolates for hanging on the tree, and miniature toys. Dozens of trees, decked out in color-coordinated decorations or thematically related baubles, such as farm animals, musical instruments, or shimmering fish, line the narrow aisles and hang from the ceiling. But the shop's real claim to fame is the glass ornaments, which are available in dozens of shapes, from traditional

The indoor Christmas market in Zurich's main train station distracts many travelers.

angels, Santas, and stars, to more unique old-time radios, monkeys riding bikes, airplanes, dice, castles, and clowns.

Also in Basel is the famous Läckerli-Huus (Leckerli House). While a variety of sweets and other gifts can be bought here, the shop, as its name implies, features the local specialty—Leckerli, a chewy spiced cookie of almond, honey, dried fruit, and kirsch. This cookie, sure to please any sweet tooth, has been made in Basel since the 1300's, when sugar was still unknown in Europe. And the proprietors of Läckerli-Huus boast that they have not changed their recipe since those days of more than 600 years ago. At Christmastime, Läckerli-Huus also sells Hypokras, a spiced wine that is especially popular with Basel residents during the holidays. In addition to its renowned goodies, the shop carries an impressive line of decorative canisters and other truly Swiss gifts. But if the Leckerli and other gifts do not attract the passers-by during the Christmas holiday season, the storefront surely does. Toward the end of November, Läckerli-Huus joins other merchants in bedecking its shop with colorful lights and fanciful decorations.

The warmly lighted Augustinergasse (the Augustinians' passage) in Zurich.

Celebrating the New Year and Other Holiday Traditions

Although Christmas is the focus of the winter holiday season, celebrating the New Year brings many Swiss to the streets in spectacular pageants of tradition and fun. The winter holiday season also includes a number of festivals that commemorate the harvest and the coming of winter. For example, November brings such harvest festivals as Bern's onion market and the sugar beet festival in Richterswil. The holiday season comes to a close with the celebration of the feast of the Epiphany, on January 6, commemorating the arrival of the Three Wise Men in Bethlehem to pay their respects to the infant Jesus.

The Glacier Express takes passengers on an exhilarating journey amidst the mountains.

Most onions bring tears to people's eyes, but not these decorated examples found in Bern's Zibelemärit, or onion market. Hundreds of farmers take part in the open-air market held on the fourth Monday of November.

New Year's Eve is often called *Silvester* in Swiss-German-speaking Switzerland, as it is the feast day of St. Silvester (also Sylvester). And in certain areas of Switzerland, the New Year arrives twice—on January 1 and again on January 13. The extra New Year's Day is a throwback to the time when people followed the Julian calendar, which was adopted in 46 B.C. by Julius Caesar and used throughout the Western world for more than 1,500 years. But after all that time, it had lost step with the solar year. To bring the calendar back in line, Pope Gregory instituted the Gregorian calendar, the one most people use today. But certain Protestant areas of Europe, including some villages in the east of Switzerland, refused to adopt the Gregorian calendar, instead clinging to the old Julian calendar for centuries. As a result, these villages acknowledge the New Silvester on December 31, and the Old Silvester on January 12.

In the city of Zurich, schoolchildren celebrate yet another Silvester—School Silvester. This Silvester comes a bit earlier than the oth-

ers, occurring on the last day of school before Christmas break. On this day, the children awaken very early and hit the streets running. They set off fireworks, ring cow bells, and hit pan lids together as cymbals, all in an effort to make as much noise as they possibly can.

New Year's customs

Whenever the Swiss celebrate it, New Year's is a festive time in Switzerland. In the fashionable ski resorts, such as Gstaad and St. Moritz, jet-set parties make it a glittering, high-class affair, while joyful processions of torch-bearing skiers winding down the slopes add an

People in the town of Saas-Fee, in the canton of Valais, observe a New Year's Eve brightened by burning torches and fireworks.

Ski Resorts

Switzerland is known for its mountains, and the Swiss Alps—part of the largest mountain system in Europe—make the country a natural place for Alpine skiing. Alpine skiing refers to skiing downhill. The term *Alpine* comes from *Alps,* the mountains in which downhill skiing originated. Downhill skiers especially enjoy the ski runs in Switzerland because most of the runs have been built at such high elevations that trees don't grow there. Snowboarding and cross-country skiing are also popular in Switzerland. Many champion skiers were born in Switzerland or use Swiss resorts to train for competition.

Swiss winter tourism developed after 1864, when a hotelkeeper at St. Moritz persuaded summer tourists from the United Kingdom to return at Christmastime. Four aristocratic families came. They loved the Alpine winter and later organized such activities as sledge racing and artistic skating. Skiing in Switzerland was known as early as the 1800's, and organized skiing is dated to 1893. Christof Iselin, a lieutenant in the Swiss army, organized a skis-versus-snowshoes race in that year, including uphill, flat, and downhill sections, to prove that skis were faster. Iselin was from Glarus, and the racers traveled from Glarus to Schwyz. The skiers made better time in all but the uphill sections!

Today, many famous Swiss ski resorts attract tourists from around the world, as well as Swiss natives. About a third of Switzerland's people ski. Slopes are rated by difficulty, so that skiers and snowboarders from beginners to experts can find a slope that fits their level of expertise. Instructors are available for lessons, and rental skis and other equipment are easy to find. The Christmas season is a very busy time for Swiss ski resorts, and some resorts are in locations that can provide winter sports year-round.

Probably the most famous of Switzerland's ski resorts is St. Moritz. Located in the far southeast region of the country in the canton of Graubünden, this resort is known for catering to celebrities and wealthy guests. St. Moritz hosted the Olympic Winter Games in 1928 and 1948. It has 50 miles (80 kilometers) of ski runs. Ski resorts operate at a number of other places in Graubünden as well, including Davos and Klosters. Many cross-country ski trails can also be found in Graubünden.

Another popular Swiss ski destination is the area around Zermatt, in the Valais canton adjacent to the Italian border. The village of Zermatt lies in a valley at the foot of the famous Matterhorn. The many mountain restaurants and the cafes and nightclubs in town make Zermatt a popular vacation spot. Snowpark Zermatt, south of the town, caters to snowboarders and freestyle skiers and is open nearly year-round. Other popular ski destinations in the Valais canton include Saas-Fee, Crans-Montana, and Verbier.

Farther north, in the Bern canton, the resort area at Gstaad features skiing up to about 10,000 feet (3,000 meters) high in the Alps. This region, through which the Saane River flows, is known as Saanenland. Picturesque chalet villages and farms dot the landscape. Winter sports schools in the region train skiers and snowboarders from beginners to experts.

Cross-country skiers in the town of Kandersteg, in the canton of Bern.

unmatched beauty to the celebration. In cities, people celebrate in restaurants or at parties, while in rural areas bonfires burn. In Geneva, people gather at the Cathédral-St-Pierre to hear *la Clémence,* its old bell, pealing in the New Year. After midnight, people wish one another well and dance in the square.

Many families celebrate New Year's Day with another special feast, often featuring the traditional New Year's loaf called *Birewegge,* or pear roll, a sweet dough filled with a dark filling of dried pears

The Swiss New Year's celebration would not be complete without the braided bread called Zopf.

and spices. Many people visit their friends and neighbors, showing up with a jug of *Hypokras,* a mulled combination of red and white wines, spices, sugar, and cloves named after the father of medicine, Hippocrates.

Special breads are traditional New Year's treats. A braided bread called *Zopf* is quite popular. Some residents of the half-canton of Nidwalden in central Switzerland may serve a spiced dough sweetened with honey and filled with gingerbread and candied citrus rind. The New Year's bread typical of the canton of Thurgau is a puff pastry with an apple-and-raisin filling. And in the valley of the Rhine River in northern Switzerland, bakers proudly present a loaf brimming with ground hazelnuts, dried fruit, and honey.

New Year's processions

The Swiss fondness for boisterous displays on their festival days extends, of course, to the celebration of the New Year. Some of the most colorful and unusual New Year's customs take place in the commu-

A fancifully dressed member of the Swiss Lifesaving Society, part of the International Lifesaving Federation, leaps into the Reuss River in the city of Lucerne as part of a New Year's celebration. In the background, is the Kapellbrücke, or Chapel Bridge, a footbridge across the Reuss originally built in the 1300's.

Chläusefieber, or Chlaus fever, strikes the small village of Urnäsch in the canton of Appenzell on New Year's Day. The cherished tradition of Silvesterkläuse finds even the youngest Swiss dressed and ready for the celebration.

nity of Laupen in the canton of Bern, in the St. Gallen village of Wil, and in Urnäsch and other communities in the canton of Appenzell.

On New Year's Eve in Laupen, schoolboys gather at the castle, excited for the start of the *Achetringele,* roughly translated as the "downhill ringing of large bells." Some of the boys, equipped with large bells, are the Achetringele themselves. Others take the role of *Bäsemanne,* or "broom men," and carry long poles festooned with juniper branches. But perhaps the luckiest of all are the *Blaateremannli,* "bladder men," who carry bouquets of pigs' bladders inflated with air. Thus outfitted, the boys set off for the town center. Along the way, the leader of the procession greets spectators with friendly rhyming wishes for a happy New Year, while the broom men wave their brooms. When the procession has ended, the real fun begins as the paraders begin to pummel the onlookers with the pigs' bladders,

Participants and onlookers at the
Silvesterkläuse in Urnäsch.

paying special attention to the young girls.

This custom originated in the early 1800's, at which time it took place on Christmas. No one knows for sure the origins of the specific roles. But because of its rowdy, irreverent character, church and town officials tried unsuccessfully to have it banned. Instead, the date was switched to New Year's Eve.

Another New Year's procession, the *Silvesterumzug* of Wil, originated in the statutory lantern inspection required long ago. At that time, officials, accompanied by lantern bearers, would inspect all houses for emergency lighting every New Year's Eve. Nowadays, at six o'clock in the evening, the lights of the town are turned down and hundreds of children play the role of the lantern bearers. Attended by drummers, the children proceed through the town carrying homemade

Several Schöne, or pretty, Chläuse pose for a moment along their route to show off their costumes. The cowbells they shoulder can weigh as much as 30 pounds each (above). Other pretty Chläuse dress as womenfolk complete with rosy-cheeked masks and towering headdresses (above, left).

lanterns. They stop three times to sing carols with accompaniment by the town band. At the end of the evening, each participating child receives a pastry. The next evening, judges award prizes to the best lanterns.

In the Aargau village of Hallwil, the people celebrate New Year's Eve with the custom of Silvestertrösche that touchingly combines pre-Christian noisemaking with Christian reverence. On the hill overlooking the village, in the orange glow of a huge bonfire, the villagers gather. At 10 minutes before midnight, eight men begin to beat rhythmically on a threshing board, an old-fashioned tool used to separate grain from chaff. Seconds before midnight the men stop, and everyone listens to the church bells ringing in the New

Year. When the bells fall silent, the men resume beating with even greater vigor. Fifteen minutes or so of this racket is believed to be sufficient to drive away the evil spirits for the rest of the year.

The Silvesterkläuse of Urnäsch

Perhaps the most elaborate New Year's procession of all takes place in the small community of Urnäsch in the canton of Appenzell. In certain households there, Christmas may come and go without much fanfare. Instead the festive days may find the man of the house tromping through the woods collecting moss and greenery, or hunched over a large plywood and cardboard object, painstakingly sewing on thousands of small glass pearls. This man—and many like him—is overcome by *Chläusefieber,* or Chlaus fever, the mixture of excitement and performance jitters that grips participants in the annual New Year's custom of the *Silvesterkläuse,* or *Chläuse* for short.

The Silvesterkläuse is a cherished tradition in Urnäsch and a handful of other Appenzell villages, including Herisau, Schwellbrunn, Hundwil, Stein, Schönengrund, and Waldstatt. However, the men of Urnäsch proudly consider their performance of the custom the purest and most artful. In the Chläuse, groups of men dressed in ornate costumes and carrying enormous bells parade through the town and countryside on the modern New Year's Eve, December 31, and on January 12, the old New Year's Eve according to the Julian calendar. The men stop at the homes of their friends, town notables, and others who appreciate the Chläuse, where they put on a performance of rhythmic bell ringing and *Zäuerli,* the yodeling that is typical of that region. Although children and adolescent boys also take part, women do not: Chläuse is strictly for men.

Early on the morning of New Year's Eve, the participants begin the preparations for their long day. First they put on their costumes. There are three types of Chläuse. The costumes of the *Schöne,* or pretty, Chläuse are the most ornate. Some pretty Chläuse dress as men folk, with velvet jackets and britches, white stockings, and clean hiking boots. Their faces are covered by a pink-faced mask, and a black pipe known as *Lendauerli* hangs from its lips. The men folk carry two

enormous cowbells weighing as much as 30 pounds each, one at the front, one at the back, slung over their shoulders with leather straps.

Other Chläuse do their best to earn their title of "pretty" by dressing as womenfolk. A velvet skirt covered by a white apron, a velvet vest over a puffy white blouse bedecked with red bows, long white gloves, and white stockings make up the ensemble. The accompanying mask is a smiling, rosy-cheeked doll face with a flower painted at the corner of the mouth. The men dressed as womenfolk carry a rack of 13 round bells, called a *Rolleträger*, similar to harness bells.

Perhaps the most spectacular item of the pretty Chläuse costumes is the headdress. It is 4 to 5 feet wide and towers 2 to 3 feet high. The outside is decorated with foil, mirrors, and thousands of glass beads. On the headdress is a scene depicting some important aspect of everyday life in the area. These headdresses are often true works of art, representing two or three years of planning and hundreds of hours of work.

On the other end of the spectrum are the *Wüeschti,* or ugly Chläuse. These men cover old clothes with natural materials such as snail shells, bark, leaves, moss, pine and juniper branches, pine cones, and nuts. Some cover their faces with vegetation. But others sculpt frightening papier-mâché demon masks complete with sharp teeth and red eyes.

The *Schö-Wüeschti,* or less-ugly Chläuse, are a relatively recent phenomenon. While the less-uglies use natural materials as do the uglies, they arrange them for a decorative effect. The first less-ugly Chläuse groups appeared in the 1960's.

Thus costumed, the Chläuse set out. When they reach a home at which they want to perform, they begin to ring their bells. The ringing is a musical endeavor, with particular rhythms and patterns that the most serious Chläuse groups rehearse diligently to perfect. Then the bells are gradually silenced, and the Chläuse sing one or more Zäuerli. This singing is also a skill. And Appenzellers, appreciating fine singers, offer the Chläuse warm drinks, which they sip through their masks with a bent straw. As the Chläuse depart, they often receive a few Swiss francs.

Although participants and aficionados are fond of describing the

Silvesterkläuse as an ancient fertility rite, no one knows the actual origins of the custom. It is known that it goes back at least to the 1600's, when church officials criticized the superstitious custom of "walking around at night with bells and making noise." Documents from the 1700's indicate that the Chläuse did not have many fans among the government officials, either. The state council issued a decree in 1744 stating that the "obscene and aggravating disguisement on the occasion of the so-called Klausen at Christmas and New Year will be forbidden and punished." This antipathy persisted into the 1900's. It was only after the 1920's that the public began to appreciate the custom.

Berchtold's Day

January 2 brings the celebration of *Berchtoldstag,* or Berchtold's Day, in some parts of Switzerland. In certain regions, this day was traditionally celebrated as a nut festival. Children began collecting nuts in

Residents of Hallwil celebrate the Bärzelitag on January 2. Dressed in costume, participants wreak havoc on their own village and then share the joy with neighboring communities. The mischief ends with a meal shared by all.

The Wise Men make their appearance on Epiphany, January 6, in many villages, towns, and cities of Switzerland. Along their way they often collect money for charity.

late autumn, and when Berchtold's Day came, they played nut games, feasted on nut goodies, sang, and performed folk dances. In other areas, neighborhood processions, meals in local pubs, and general merriment were the order of the day.

In Hallwil, January 2 is the *Bärzelitag,* and the celebration has elements of a pre-Christian spring-renewal ritual. Fifteen young, unmarried adults dress in costumes and masks—five as the "green," five as the "parched brown," and the remaining five as a camel and its drivers. During the day, the costumed groups run through the village, pulling pranks. When they have exhausted all opportunities for mischief in their own village, they make similar runs in neighboring towns. The day ends with a meal shared by all.

Epiphany

Epiphany is an important celebration in Catholic Switzerland. But even this holy day has a pre-Christian connection. In ancient times, the 12 *Rauchnächte* (literally, "smoke nights"), which were nights when the spirits supposedly rose and wandered the earth, ended on January 6. Households and churches celebrate Epiphany by adding the final element to their nativity scenes—figures of the Three Wise Men. In many cities, towns, and villages today, men dressed as the Wise Men collect money for charity on that day. Recently, modern-day Wise Men in Basel collected more than $35,000, to benefit a children's hospital.

On Epiphany, many families bake a special sweet bread called *Gâteau des Rois* (kings' cake) in French and *Dreikönigskuche* (three-kings' cake) in Swiss-German. This loaf is made by sticking together lumps of dough before baking so that it comes hot from the oven as a ring of easy-to-separate rolls. Inside one of the rolls is a little token—a plastic crown, king, Madonna, or other figure. The lucky diner who receives the roll with the token has the privilege of wearing a crown and is promised good luck for the whole year.

In Ticino, some families celebrate the Epiphany the Italian way, with a visit from Befana. According to legend, Befana was an old lady—some accounts say a witch—whom the Three Wise

Below, a Gâteau des Rois (kings' cake), the traditional sweet bread for the Epiphany. Made of individual balls of dough stuck together before baking, there is no doubt that this treat is fit for a king.

Men approached for directions to Bethlehem. But Befana was so engrossed in her household chores that she could not put her broom down for even a moment to help them. No sooner had they gone on their way, though, than poor Befana began to feel ashamed that she had not helped them. She set out after them but never caught up with them. To this day, she roams the world at Epiphany giving gifts to well-behaved children and punishing the naughty ones with whacks from her broom. In some households, the children anticipate Befana's visit by hanging a *stivale,* or boot, by the fireplace. Befana comes down the chimney and fills the stivale with presents.

So ends the season

While Epiphany is the official end of the Christmas season in Switzerland, perhaps it is fitting to mention one final holy day: the *Festa di San Antonio,* the Feast of Saint Anthony, which celebrates the humble beasts of the earth. On January 17, in the canton of Ticino, farmers bring their animals to church for a blessing. From the donkeys and horses ridden by St. Nicholas and pulling his sleigh; to the barnyard animals who supposedly talk on Christmas Eve; to the ox, lamb, and cow that paid the first respects to the newborn baby Jesus, animals have their part in the Christmas celebration. Perhaps the Feast of St. Anthony can be interpreted as a way to make sure their contributions—at Christmas and throughout the year—are not overlooked.

Swiss Crafts

Jingle Bell Wreath

You can bring the Swiss traditon of bells into your home by making a wreath out of shiny jingle bells.

Materials

- 33 jingle bells*, 0.60 inches (15 mm) diameter
- 1 pipe cleaner, $\frac{5}{32}$ inch (4 mm) diameter, 12 inches (30 cm) long
- ribbon
- scissors

1. Thread the bells in alternating positions on the pipe cleaner, as shown, so the bells fit snugly next to each other.

2. When all of the bells have been added, twist the ends of the pipe cleaner together to close the circle.

3. Finish the wreath by tying a loop of ribbon around the connected ends of the pipe cleaner to make a hanger. Add a big bow for the final festive touch!

The hoop on the jingle bell should look like this.

Clothespin Star

Brighten any spot with this easy-to-make clothespin star.

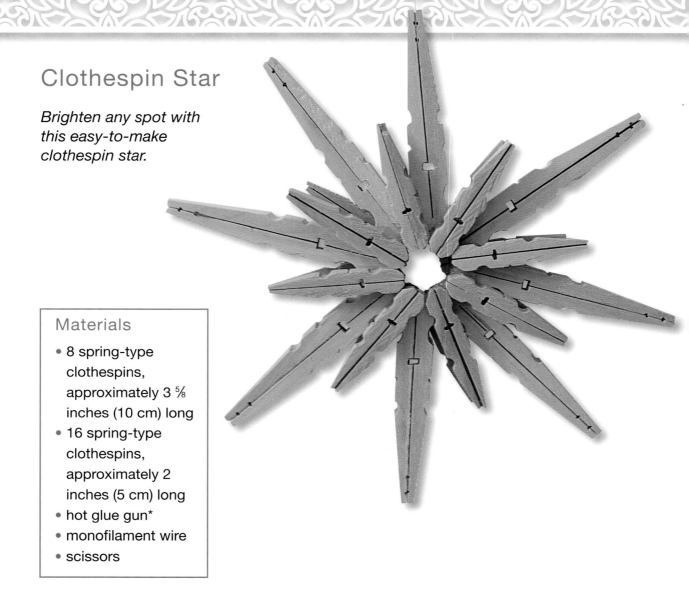

Materials

- 8 spring-type clothespins, approximately 3 ⅝ inches (10 cm) long
- 16 spring-type clothespins, approximately 2 inches (5 cm) long
- hot glue gun*
- monofilament wire
- scissors

1. Remove the springs from the clothespins. Glue a clothespin together as shown. Be sure to work over a covered surface in case the glue drips. Repeat for all of the clothespins.

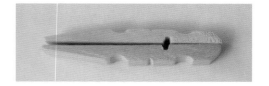

*Ask a grown-up to help when using the hot glue gun.

2. Arrange the large clothespins in a circle on a flat, covered surface. Remove one clothespin at a time and apply the hot glue to the inside top edges. Return the clothespin to the circle by attaching it to its neighbor. Repeat with the remaining large clothespins. Let the glue dry.

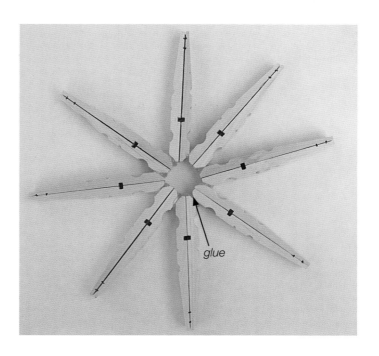

glue

3. Glue the smaller clothespins to the top of the large clothespin circle, as shown. After the glue has dried, repeat this step on the other side.

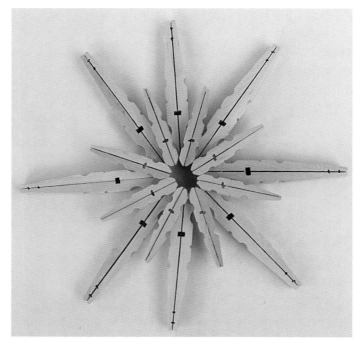

4. To finish off the star, thread a piece of monofilament wire through an opening in one of the clothespins. Tie the ends to create a loop.

Pine Cone Pixies

Just as the Swiss use decorations from nature, you can use a pine cone to create Christmas cheer.

1. Use these images as patterns and trace them on the tracing paper. Then, enlarge the patterns by as much as 200%. Cut out the enlarged patterns and place them on the felt. Cut around the paper patterns to create your felt pieces.

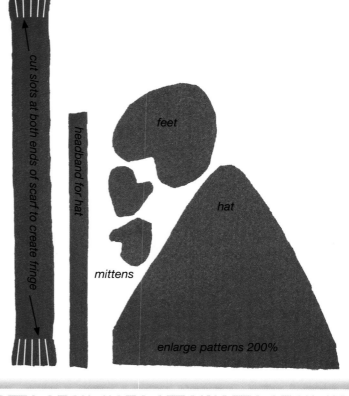

cut slots at both ends of scarf to create fringe

headband for hat

feet

hat

mittens

enlarge patterns 200%

Materials

- tracing paper
- fine-tip black marker
- red, green, or gray felt
- scissors
- pine cone approximately 3 inches (8 cm) high with a base diameter of approximately 2 ½ inches (6 cm)
- round wooden ball, 1 ¼ inches (3 cm) diameter with a pre-drilled hole
- hot glue gun*
- small jingle bell
- toothpicks
- pale pink marker
- seasonal items, such as red berries, greens, ribbon, stars, etc.

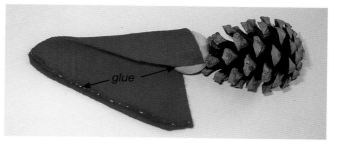

3. To make the hat, glue the felt onto the ball by placing a dot of hot glue in the middle of the base of the hat, and press it onto what will be the forehead of the pixie. Place a dot of glue on the pointed corner and press to the back of the ball. Place a line of glue along the free side of the felt, as shown. Roll the pine cone toward the glued edge to press the seam together. Hold in place until the glue has dried.

2. Position the ball on top of the pine cone so that the most attractive side of the cone and ball face forward and the tip of the pine cone is inside the hole in the ball. Working over a covered surface, hot glue the wooden ball to the top of the pine cone. Let the glue dry completely.

Glue the headband to the base of the hat, placing the seam at the back. Bend the tip of the hat toward one side and place a dot of glue in the fabric bend. Hold in place until the glue dries.

Finish the hat by either sewing or gluing a small jingle bell to the tip.

*Ask a grown-up to help when using the hot glue gun.

4. Fold the scarf along the length of the felt and wrap it around to one side of the neck. Secure each end with glue. Unfold the fringed ends of the scarf.

glue

glue the mittens to the sides

glue the feet to the base

5. Before gluing the feet to the base of the pine cone, test to see if it leans. If so, you can glue part of a toothpick in between the cone and the felt to straighten it.

6. Glue the mittens to each side of the pine cone. You can add small seasonal items, such as berries or a bow so that the pixie has something to hold.

7. Lastly, draw eyes and a mouth with a fine-tip black marker. Use a pale pink marker to add rosy cheeks.

Swiss Recipes

Capretto (Roasted Kid)

2 tbsp. butter
1 tsp. ground sage
1 tbsp. fresh mint
¼ tsp. cinnamon
⅛ tsp. nutmeg

2 lbs. boneless kid (young goat),
    cut into bite-sized pieces
salt and pepper to taste
1 cup sherry
1 cup cream
1 tbsp. rum

Melt the butter in a Dutch oven over medium heat. Add the sage, mint, cinnamon, and nutmeg and stir for 3 minutes. Sprinkle the meat with salt and pepper to taste and toss to coat. Add the meat to the butter mixture and brown on all sides. Lower the heat and add the sherry. Simmer, covered, until the meat is tender. Remove the meat and keep warm. Add the cream and rum to the Dutch oven; stir well. Bring mixture to a boil and continue to boil until mixture is reduced by a third. Serve the meat on a bed of rice and top with sauce. Makes 4 to 6 servings.

Cheese Fritters

¼ tsp. white pepper
2 well-beaten eggs
½ lb. Gruyère cheese, cut into 12 1-inch cubes
¾ cup breadcrumbs
vegetable oil for deep frying

Add pepper to beaten eggs. Dip cheese cubes into eggs and then into breadcrumbs. Repeat. Fry in oil for 1 to 2 minutes or until golden brown, turning once. Remove with a slotted spoon, allowing excess oil to drain off. Serve immediately with festive toothpicks. Makes 6 servings.

Onion Tart

Dough
2 cups presifted all-purpose flour
¼ tsp. salt
½ cup shortening
4 tbsp. ice water

Filling
2 tbsp. butter
10 medium onions, thinly sliced
salt and pepper to taste
1 cup milk
1 cup cream
3 tbsp. flour
2 eggs, well beaten
1 cup Swiss cheese, shredded

To make the dough, combine the flour and salt. Cut in the shortening until particles the size of small peas form. Add water. Stir to form a stiff dough. Knead dough on a lightly floured surface. Roll out to fit a buttered 14-inch pie pan. Prick dough with a fork. Set aside.

To make the filling, melt the butter in a large skillet; add the onions and salt and pepper to taste. Sauté the onions until golden brown. In a medium bowl combine the milk and cream. Gradually add the flour; blend until smooth. Beat in the eggs and cheese. Add the sautéed onions.

Pour the filling into the dough-lined pan. Bake in a preheated 350 °F oven 30 minutes. Raise oven temperature to 400 °F and bake 5 minutes longer or until the top is browned. Serve immediately. Makes 6 servings.

Mixed Greens with Roquefort Dressing

3 cups tightly packed torn red-leaf lettuce
3 cups tightly packed torn Boston lettuce
2 cups tightly packed torn endive
2 cups loosely packed trimmed watercress
½ cup cucumber, peeled and thinly sliced
½ cup celery, chopped
1 tbsp. fresh parsley, chopped
¼ tsp. salt
⅛ tsp. freshly ground pepper
¼ tsp. dry mustard
3 tbsp. red wine vinegar
1 tbsp. water
1 tbsp. olive oil
2 tbsp. Roquefort cheese, crumbled
1 small red pepper, cut into small squares

Combine salad greens, cucumber, and celery in a large bowl; toss gently.

Combine parsley, salt, pepper, mustard, vinegar, water, and oil in a small bowl; stir with a wire whisk until well blended. Add crumbled cheese and blend further. Pour dressing over mixed salad greens, tossing gently to coat. Garnish with red pepper. Makes 6 servings.

Muesli

3 tbsp. quick-cooking oatmeal
3 tbsp. water
1 tbsp. fresh lemon juice
1 tbsp. honey
1 large apple
1 tbsp. almonds

Make the oatmeal according to the package directions, using 3 tablespoons of oatmeal and water; add more water or oats to get the consistency you prefer. Stir in the lemon juice and honey. Grate the apple, skin and all, into the muesli. Stir in almonds. Feel free to use any fresh fruit to replace the apple. Makes 1 serving.

Basler Brunsli (Chocolate~Almond Cookies)

2 cups ground almonds, divided
1¼ cups granulated sugar
1 cup grated semi-sweet chocolate
1 tsp. cinnamon
½ tsp. ground cloves
2 egg whites, lightly beaten

Combine 1½ cups almonds with sugar, chocolate, cinnamon, and cloves in a large mixing bowl. Add egg whites. Knead the mixture to form a stiff dough. If the mixture is too sticky, add more almonds as necessary. If the mixture crumbles, add water, 1 teaspoon at a time, until the consistency is right.

On a surface lightly coated with granulated sugar, press the dough to ¼-inch thickness. Cut out cookies with a heart-shaped cookie cutter dipped in granulated sugar; place on cookie sheets lined with greased aluminum foil. Allow cookies to stand at room temperature for about 2 hours. Bake cookies in preheated 300 °F oven 15 minutes. Cool on wire racks; store in an airtight container. Makes 2 to 3 dozen cookies.

Anisbrötli (Anise Cookies)

3 eggs
1½ cups sugar
2 tbsp. aniseed
grated rind of one lemon

2 cups all-purpose flour
1 tsp. baking powder

Beat the eggs until light. Gradually add sugar, beating well after each addition. Continue to beat mixture for 15 minutes. Stir in aniseed and grated lemon rind. In a separate bowl, sift the flour with the baking powder. Gradually add flour mixture to form a stiff dough. Knead dough on a lightly floured surface, then cut into four equal pieces. Roll each piece into strips, 1 inch thick. Cut strips into 3-inch lengths. Nick each strip 3 times to the depth of ½ inch. Shape strips into U's, keeping the nicked edge outside. Place the cookies on greased cookie sheets. Allow to stand overnight at room temperature. Bake in a preheated 300 °F oven 15 minutes. Makes 2 dozen cookies.

Mailänderli (Christmas Butter Cookies)

1 cup unsalted butter, softened
½ cup sugar
grated rind of 1 lemon
juice of 1 lemon

3 eggs
2½ cups presifted all-purpose flour
1 egg yolk, well beaten

In a large bowl, cream butter and sugar until light and fluffy. Add grated lemon rind and lemon juice. Beat in eggs, one at a time, mixing well after each addition. Gradually stir in flour. Knead the dough until it is smooth and not sticky. If it is too sticky, add small amounts of flour until it clears the fingers. Wrap the dough in plastic wrap and chill overnight.

Roll out the dough between two pieces of waxed paper to a ¼-inch thickness. Cut the dough with small cookie cutters. Place cookies on greased, floured cookie sheets. Brush with beaten egg yolk. Bake in a preheated 350 °F oven about 12 to 15 minutes, or until golden. Store cookies in an airtight container. Makes 4 dozen cookies.

Spicy Pear Roll

1 lb. dried pears
⅓ cup red wine (if desired)
1 tbsp. unsalted butter (if desired)
½ cup brown sugar
½ lb. seedless red grapes, coarsely chopped
¾ cup figs, coarsely chopped
¼ cup candied lemon peel, coarsely chopped

½ cup walnut pieces
1 tsp. cinnamon
½ tsp. ground cloves
¼ cup kirsch (approximately)
bread dough (recipe below)
2 well-beaten eggs

Place pears in a large saucepan. Add water to cover; soak overnight. Pour off all but ¼ cup of the water. Coarsely chop the pears and return to the pan. Add red wine and butter, if desired. Simmer, covered, over low heat until pears are tender and most of the liquid has evaporated, about 10 minutes. Add sugar, grapes, figs, lemon peel, walnuts, cinnamon, and cloves; blend thoroughly. Stir in enough kirsch to form a thick jam.

Punch down the bread dough until it falls, and divide in two. On a lightly floured surface, roll out each to a 12-inch square; spread with filling, leaving ¾-inch edges. Roll up the bread, gently sealing the edge with water. Brush the top of the roll with beaten egg. Place on a greased cookie sheet. Allow to rise until doubled in size. Bake in a preheated 350 °F oven 30 minutes or until golden brown. Cool before cutting. Makes 2 loaves.

Dough for Spicy Pear Roll

2 packages active dry yeast
½ tsp. sugar
½ cup lukewarm water
¼ cup unsalted butter
¾ cup milk

½ cup sugar
1 tsp. salt
1 egg, well beaten
5 cups bread flour

Dissolve yeast and ½ teaspoon sugar in the lukewarm water; set aside. Heat together butter and milk until the butter melts; pour into a large bowl and add sugar, salt, and egg. Allow mixture to cool. Stir in dissolved yeast. Add enough flour to form a soft dough. Knead dough on a lightly floured surface. Return dough to bowl; cover and allow to rise in a warm place until doubled in size, about 1 hour.

Swiss Carols

Tedlei, O Fideivels
(O Come, All Ye Faithful)

J. F. Wade

Andante moderato

1. Ted - lei, o fi - dei - vels,
2. Bein spert cun pre - mu - ra
3. Na - dal, o fi - dei - vels,

la le - grei - vla no - va: na - schius ei il
da lur mun - ta ne - ras ar - ri - van tiel
tgei le - grei - vla fia - sta! Ve - gni tuts, vo -

Se - gner a Bet - le - hem.
Se - gner ils buns pa - sturs.
gni cun grond le - gher - ment!

Leu sur la stal - la con - tan - mel - li
O tgei le - gri - a, igl af - fon els
Il car Sal - va - der nus tuts be - ne -

aun - ghels:
an - flan: Ve - ni te, a - do - re - mus, ve - ni - te, a - do -
de - scha:

re - mus, ve - ni - te, a - do - re - mus Do - mi - num.

The Star of Bethlehem Shines Bright

Music and Text by Paul Burkhard

Andante

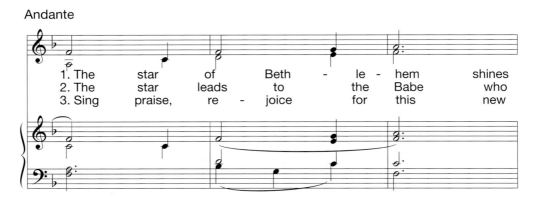

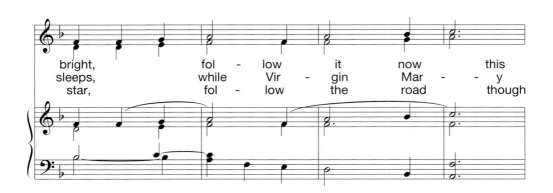

"The Star of Bethlehem Shines Bright" from A Swiss Nativity: Christmas Play with Music by Paul Burkhard © 1965 by Musikverlag Und Bühnenvertrieb Zürich AG; English translation by Eleanor Gurewitsch. Reprinted with permission of Musikverlag Und Bühnenvertrieb Zürich AG.

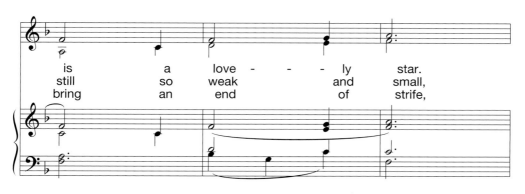

is a love - - ly star.
still so weak and small,
bring an end of strife,

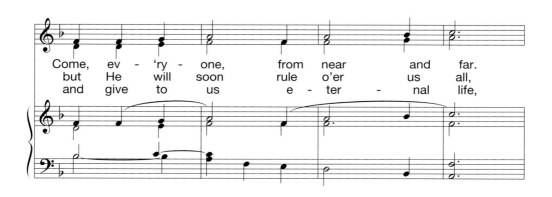

Come, ev - 'ry - one, from near and far.
but He will soon rule o'er us all,
and give to us e - ter - nal life,

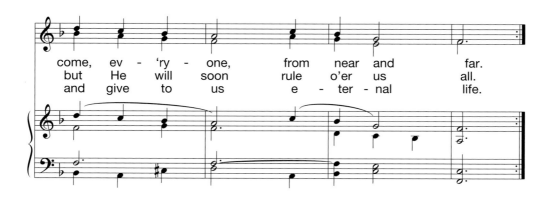

come, ev - 'ry - one, from near and far.
but He will soon rule o'er us all.
and give to us e - ter - nal life.

Acknowledgments

Cover	© Siegfried Eigstler, Getty Images
2	© Anshar/Shutterstock
5	© Mihai-Bogdan Lazar, Shutterstock
6	© Prisma Bildagentur AG/Alamy Images
12	© Peter Schneider, Keystone/AP Photo; © Alexander Chaikin, Shutterstock
10	WORLD BOOK map
11	© Juan Moyano, Alamy Images
12	© Godong/Alamy Images
14	© Alessandro Della Bella, Keystone/AP Photo
16	© Godong/Alamy Images
17	© Christof Sonderegger, Prisma/SuperStock
18	© Prisma Bildagentur AG/Alamy Images
20	© GFC Collection/Alamy Images
21	© Quanthem/Shutterstock
23	© Lapina Anna, Shutterstock; © Ivonne Wierink, Shutterstock
25	© Joana Kruse, Alamy Images
26	© Prisma Bildagentur AG/Alamy Images
27	© Manfred Glueck, Alamy Images
28	© Viktor1/Shutterstock
29	© Alessandro Colle, Shutterstock
30	© Travelstock44/Alamy Images
33	© Elquest/Shutterstock
34	© Prisma Bildagentur AG/Alamy Images
36	© Engler Stephan, Prisma/SuperStock
37	© Hemis/Alamy Images
38	© Stohler Fotos
39	© Westend61 GmbH/Alamy Images
40	© Antonio Violi, Alamy Images
41	© Denis Linine, Shutterstock
42	© Yoko Aziz, age fotostock/SuperStock
43	© Prisma Bildagentur AG/Alamy Images
44	© Marco Mayer, Shutterstock
45	© Pierre Albouy, Reuters; © Alistair Scott, Alamy Images
46	© Travelstock44/Alamy Images
47	© FatVogel/Shutterstock
48	© Alessandro Colle, Shutterstock
50	© Prisma Bildagentur AG/Alamy Images
51	© Stephane Jaquemet, Alamy Images
53	© Sabpics/Shutterstock
54	© Ronald Sumners, Shutterstock
55	© Urs Flueeler, Keystone/AP Photo
56	© RnDmS/Shutterstock
57	© RnDmS/Shutterstock; © Fulcanelli, Shutterstock
58	© RnDmS/Shutterstock; © Fulcanelli, Shutterstock
61	© EPA/Alamy Images
62	© Fiorenzo Maffi, Reuters
63	© Arco Images GmbH/Alamy Images
65-70	WORLD BOOK photos by Brenda Tropinski
72	© Dar1930/Shutterstock
73	© Bozhena Melnyk, Shutterstock
75	© JuJik/Shutterstock